GLYPHS

Glyphs

With Poems New and Revised by

Colin B. Douglas

Waking Lion Press

Cover: *The Angel Standing in the Sun,* painting by William Turner, 1876.

ISBN 978-1-4341-0390-1

Published by Waking Lion Press, an imprint of The Editorium

Waking Lion Press™, the Waking Lion Press logo, and The Editorium™ are trademarks of The Editorium, LLC

The Editorium, LLC
West Jordan City, UT 84081-6132
wakinglionpress.com
wakinglion@editorium.com

For Linda, who is a gift from the Marvelous

Ye were also—in the beginning, with the Father— that which is
Spirit, even the Spirit of truth.
—Doctrine and Covenants 93:23

Forasmuch then as we are the offspring of God....
—Acts 17:29

Your old men shall dream dreams,
Your young men shall see visions.
—Joel 2:28

... Into the plenum of the
Community of love
—Kenneth Rexroth, The Dragon and the Unicorn

Contents

Preface

Somewhere among words
An opening
Search among words
As between a beloved's legs
Somewhere an opening
Somewhere light
Somewhere water
First Light
First Water

CREATION MYTH

That which says "I AM"—
That which is Spirit,
Even the Spirit of truth—
Knows itself first
Through the eyes of
Eternal Mother and
Eternal Father
As they look each upon the other,
And in their mutual love and desire is
Beginning.

November 2014

Another Creation Myth

A revision of the King Follett Discourse
With apologies to Joseph Smith and a nod to Eliza Snow

Eternal Man and Eternal Woman (they are the Gods) find themselves in the midst of intelligences and glory. Because they are greater, the Gods see proper to beget the lesser intelligences as their spirit children and to let Eternal Man institute laws whereby they can have a privilege to advance like themselves and be exalted with them, so that the lesser intelligences might have one glory upon another in all that knowledge, power, and glory. So they take in hand to save the world of intelligences. Eternal Man says to Eternal Woman, "Let us do so," and she answers, "That is my desire, also; let it be so"; and they couple, and she gives birth to the intelligences as their spirit children; and thus the Gods are Eternal Father and Eternal Mother.

10 January 2015

Doctrine and Covenants

Thy dominion shall be an everlasting dominion,
And without compulsory means
It shall flow unto thee forever and ever.
—D&C 121:46

Words: *matter, element, spirit, intelligence,*
light, glory, agency, male, female, God, man.
And behind the words?
Say *I* and there is *you;*
Say *light* and there is *darkness;*
Yes and there is *no.*
It comes to this:
Lover receiving lover,
Flow of seed,
Flow of light, galaxies, worlds, plants, beasts, man and woman,
Then children, tribes, cities, wars and rumors of wars,
The cross, the empty tomb, a sea of glass;
But it comes to this:
My love, I touch your face,
Your kiss is tender.
Let us lie down in the grass.

Revised March 2015

I Am Told of a Certain Tree

I am told of a certain tree,
And a certain well:
That the fruit of the tree
And the water from the well
Are unspeakably sweet;
And I have tasted fruit
No man could name,
And water whose source
No man could tell,
And, having tasted,
I know of greater folly
Than to seek that tree
And that well.

Adonai, Forsake Me Not

The Lord knoweth how to deliver the godly out of temptations
—2 Peter 2:9

Adonai, forsake me not;
turn not away.
Sin like a girl comes whispering;
like a girl with light fingers,
whispering softly.

Adonai, I Have Sinned

Touch these stones, O Lord, with thy finger
—Ether 3:4

Adonai, I have sinned;
I have sinned grievously against you.
My legs are water, my bowels burn;
my bowels are hot stone.
Silence encloses me like iron walls;
I cannot hear your voice.
I have sinned against you,
and your voice is shut out.
As you touched the small stones,
reach forth to touch me;
make me clean as burning stone.
I have loved you in time past;
I have embraced your fire.
Embrace me now in my uncleanness.

I Sought You, Adonai

Ye shall seek me, and find me
—Jeremiah 29:13

I sought you, Adonai, and I found you.
I sought you among the firs and the alders,
Among the stars of clear skies.
I found you not there.
I sought you on hilltops,
I sought you in clear streams,
In the gold and red of trout,
And I found you not there.
But in the clouded and starless night
When I sought you with tears,
When I knelt in ashes,
I found you; your finger touched me.
And now, among the firs and the alders,
Among stars and on hilltops,
In clear streams
And in the gold and red of trout,
I find you, Adonai,
I find you.

Prayer

Remember not the sins of my youth
—Psalm 25:7

Father, my sins are not hidden from you;
upon my bed I remember them.
Before my shut eyes they dance
and watch me with solemn mockery.
I would forget them;
will you not remove them?
Let there be a garden of tulips before me,
washed by spring rain;
walk in it with me.
As a raindrop on a tulip petal,
so would I be before you.

LIKE A DEER HE COMES TO ME

Take, eat: this is my body
—Mark 14:22

Like a deer he comes to me,
parting the ferns,
like a deer with bright antlers.
I chase him across meadows,
beside streams I pursue him,
and he does not weary;
But in the thicket he surprises me,
he lets my arrow pierce him.
He gives me of his flesh at evening,
and in the bright morning
like a deer he comes to me.

Adonai, Cover Me with Your Robe

That the Lord shall give thee rest
—2 Nephi 24:3

Adonai, cover me with your robe;
let me rest against you.
I have traveled in far places;
where you have sent me, I have gone.
Among serpents I have laid my bed;
I have risen to go among wolves.
I have walked in dry places
where the rocks held no water;
I have crossed high mountains
where frost was my covering.
I have gone unshod;
my feet have bled.
I am weary;
I have found no rest.
Let me rest against you;
shelter me with your robe.

Revised January 2015

The Earth upon Her Wings Moves Not So Quietly

The earth rolls upon her wings
—D&C 88:45

The earth upon her wings moves not so quietly
As He walks in corridors of light.
Morning mists, the bloom of flowers,
Air still on meadows—
More quietly than these He goes.

The Grasses Sing and the Trees Shout

Behold, and lo, the Bridegroom cometh
—D&C 88:92

The grasses sing and the trees shout
as Shaddai descends to receive his bride.
The stones laugh and the rivers leap;
as he kisses her mouth, the clouds rain wine.
In the meadows of Eden he lies with her,
and the issue of her womb is heavenly lights.

LET THE STONE WHISPER TO THE FLOWER

Behold, and lo, the Bridegroom cometh
—D&C 88:92

Let the stone whisper to the flower,
The flower to the sun,
And the sun to the stars of heaven,
That Jehovah is come for his bride;
She bends her knee graciously to him.
The sun hides its face,
And all silvering clouds, all shimmering snow
Are darkness to the light of her raiment.
He calls her Zion;
He lifts her by the hand.
The stone whispers to the flower
And the flower to the sun
That his kiss is tender.
The table is set; the wine is served;
And the stars break forth in song.

A Daughter of Sarah Is My Beloved

If a man marry a wife…by the new and everlasting covenant
—D&C 132:19

A daughter of Sarah is my beloved,
a priestess in Abraham's house.
Her knee is bent to the Lord;
she dwells within the circle of his law.
For virtue she is clean as rain,
as streams that descend high slopes.
Her smile is as sunlight on meadows,
her speech a sparrow's flight for gentleness.
Her counsel is heard in the congregation;
to the ears of the wise she speaks wisdom.
She gives bread to those who have not asked;
the afflicted receive comfort at her hand.
Her love she has not withheld from me;
she has given me all delights.
Sons and daughters she has given me;
our generations will fill the heavens.
Our covenant will stand forever;
beyond death I shall know her embrace.
Though the earth melt at His coming,
I shall never be parted from her.

My Beloved Shall Be Mine beyond Death

If a man marry a wife... by the new and everlasting covenant
—D&C 132:19

My beloved shall be mine beyond death,
for by His sure nails we are joined.
Though our bones go down to darkness,
I shall never be parted from her.
With the just we await the dawn;
in the morning we shall rise with the sun.
Our children will gather about us;
on Mount Zion we shall stand together.
In the fields of a new earth I shall embrace her;
in the gardens of a new Eden she will receive me.
Our generations will fill the heavens,
and worlds without end will honor her.

Wedding Songs

If a man marry a wife ... by the new and everlasting covenant
—D&C 132:19

i

On the first morning of our marriage,
You gave me raspberries in a white bowl.
Later we stood barefoot on sand
And let white sea foam wash about our ankles.

ii

We lay down among flowers,
The grass sweet and wet,
Your dress wet.
Horses came near under blue sky,
Treading down the sweet grass,
And your dress was yellow among the flowers.

iii

The whiteness of foam,
The smell of morning rain;
And as we walked on the sand,
My fingertips touched your sleeve.

iv

I come with gifts of milk and wine,
Silver shoes, and a bough of cherries,
And enter your garden of roses.

v

Your hand through the parted veil,
And later, the forked flame of your thighs.
Sarai's limbs in Abram's tent
Could not have burned more bright.

More Wedding Songs

Who is she that looketh forth as the morning, fair as the sun, clear as the moon,
terrible as an army with banners?
—Song of Solomon 6:10

i

Flute songs float up from your hair
A tulip is one eye and a daffodil the other
Clouds of butterflies are the skin of your belly
Meadows of fresh grass are your thighs
Honeybees make a hive of your bowels
A rising sun in clear sky tips each of your fingers
A galaxy revolves in black space on each of your palms
White-water rivers cascade from beneath your toenails
Armies with bright banners gallop across a plain beyond the gateway
    of your sex

ii

I fall into you as into a dream of a house
The front doors open outward wide
I tumble through
To roll into an ocean of flowers vermillion

iii

My hands grasp your ribcage
Stars are your nipples

iv

Your ribcage holds the sun
Light streams between my fingers

v

In the orchard
Swollen fruit
Wet grass tangled
Sunlight refracted in raindrops
Shining in the veins

vi

My hands cupped about your breasts
A thumb over each nipple
Your eyes open to meet mine

September, October 2014

Deer Come Down from the Hills

Deer come down from the hills,
Down the ravines,
Dry creek beds;
Grass dry,
Wind cold.
The high hills are colder,
Dusted by snow.
Your eyes are brown as a deer's.

A Separate Peace

Wo, wo is me, the mother of men
—Moses 7:48

Earth the mother of men:
Then is not Sun,
By whose seed of light Earth conceives,
The father of men?
And Moon is sister,
And every creature brother or sister.
I greet you,
My family,
My tribe:
Father Sun,
Mother Earth,
Sister Moon,
Brother and Sister Raven,
Brother and Sister Coyote.
All creatures,
My brothers and sisters,
I weep with you,
And in the Creator
With you I hope.
Let there be peace between us.

November 2014

Deer Have Passed Here

Deer have passed here
A doe, a fawn
Maybe a buck
Those tracks are bigger
They come down in moonlight
To browse on green corn
Silent as moonlight
They pass

Revised March 2014

A Cup of Water in the High Uintahs

Snow
Granite
Spruce and quakies
Meadow
Streams
Join to become
The Duchesne
Green
Colorado
Gulf of California
Pacific
And beyond—
Here I drink
Of the Black Sea
And of rain on the Kirgiz Steppe

September 2014

Haiku

Airplane turning above mountain—
Brightness
Of steel and snow

Cirrus on blue sky—
Snow powder
Blown up from the ridge

From glacial pool
Trout
Stares back

September 2014

Low tide
Mudflat
White of empty clam shells

September 2014

On Lake Mountain

Maples red and orange
Snow on distant ridge
Wind coming somewhere off ice
Badger's white skull under juniper
My dog runs the trail
On Lake Mountain in October

October 2014

Coordinates

Feet on rock
Sun before
Moon behind
Four ravens above

November 2014

Outside the Longhouse

Early light through low clouds
Beach at low tide
Canoes drawn up
Smell of alder smoke
My woman still wrapped in a bear skin
Last night I dreamed Raven stole our fire

September 2014

Peel Back a Bit of Skin and See

Peel back a bit of skin and see
The sun blazing over stone and sand
And rivulets of light
Trickling through the crevices of fear

Luminous Books

Luminous books
A pool of fish flaming
Snow rises through the grass
What is this book that speaks
Of snow and fish and grass?

Revised January 2015

Last Night's Equations

Last night's equations are inscribed on the eyes of morning
A woman holds in her teeth the moon
As delicately as Urim balanced on the tip of a salmon's fin
The moon slips from the woman's teeth
The eyes of morning take its place
The equations float
White feathers back into the night

A Girl on the Platform

A girl on the platform
Hair of pearls floating on the wind
Turns slowly counterclockwise
Raises her right arm toward the sky
Hair of pearls floating
Speaks one unheard syllable
Inscribes a question on the wind

A Girl on a Bridge Beckons

A girl on a bridge beckons
A girl in a dress of broken glass
A girl with teeth of early snow
A girl whose legs are marble pillars on a distant hill
A girl with hair of ivy where small birds nest
A girl whose eyes are open doorways
A girl who knows what is written behind the mirror

Tangle of Roads, Houses, Seas

Tangle of roads, houses, seas
Tangle of hallways and doors and glass
A face beyond the tangled highways of the sun
Of seas and rocks and shoals and shores

I Don't Know Why the Moon Is White

For Charles Cros

I don't know why the moon is white
I don't know where the butterflies sleep
I don't know why a man leans a ladder against a white wall
Or why the wall curves gently away

Revised September 2014

A Mirror Half Hidden by Fallen Leaves

A mirror half hidden by fallen leaves
White hand extended through the glass
Deer pass through the clearing one by one
And do not leave a scrap of paper to blow
Across the grass in a hot wind
Beneath a white sun obscured by antlers
Eyes unblinking in the glare
We watch from behind a corner of a distant building
And wait to fall into the mirror

A Walk in the Woods

A walk in the woods
Leaves brown and golden
Golden towers rising above the trees
Girls on the lake shore
Naked, watchful,
Eyes of red stop lights
Swinging in the wind on a single cable
Storm rising in the east
Rain washing the towers
Plastic blowing in the wind
Wraps about the girls

The Vision of All Becomes

The vision of all becomes
As a face peering through leaves
Expressionless
Wordless
A tangle of branches and leaves
Behind them a mirror set against a tree trunk
And in the mirror a face
The trees veiled in snow
Ecstatic beneath the sun

No Memory

No memory
No feet
No eyes
No light
No darkness
No pendants flapping in the breeze
No yellow pendants
No blue pendants
No red pendants
No face looking up from beneath the surface of the water
No lovers entwined among the ferns
No book lying open beneath the sun
No voice

A Long Hallway

A long hallway
Old wallpaper
Old carpet
Musty smell
Bare dim light bulbs hanging by cords from the ceiling
Yellowed white-painted doors
Many doors both sides of the hallway
The hallway not straight
It curves gradually to the right
The line of sight cut off in the distance
Just before the lines converge
Whether the hallway makes a circle
That remains unanswered
But open a door and then another
Behind one a lilac grove
Behind another an empty room
Behind another a boulevard by the sea
And one's greatest desire after all
Is to lie down by the sea and sleep

A Girl Floats on a River of Light

A girl floats on a river of light
Blue pelican love
And the boats drawn up on the beach
Where a girl rests against the rocks
Is this how it begins?
A mist rises from the river with an agate in its teeth
Bits of rags, red and yellow
Long strips of rags wrapped about a pole
A mouth wide open
Gleaming teeth
Waves swell and crash green and white
A woman in white floats among the trees
Rain falls steadily through the night
Ten minutes from the ocean
A difficult decision
The wings of a gull curve against a clear sky
A difficult decision
This is how it begins

There Is No Interest in Pascal

There is no interest in Pascal
But sparrows flock to the bust of Zeno
The refugees scattered across the plain fear the smoke of burning lies
But their fear is containable
So long as the mothers continue their vigil behind the mountains
Tomorrow; we wait for tomorrow
Perhaps tomorrow the bust of Pascal will join the vigil

Revised December 2015

A Man Remembers

A man remembers a house in a small town, in a country of firs and much rain. He awakes one night to the sound of rain on the roof, and unable to return to sleep he rises from his bed and goes to the back door to watch the rain fall. In a puddle near the door a pale plastic doll lies naked, face up. He is alone in this house, there are no children, and so he wonders how the doll has come to be there. There was a woman in this house the night before. He stood with her in the kitchen, kissing her mouth, his right hand lifting the hem of her dress. The doll is more pink than the skin of that woman. Near the house is an apple orchard, old and neglected, the trees overgrown, apples rotting on the ground. He likes the smell of the rotting apples in the fall. Beyond the orchard stand large old fir trees, and among the trees a house, white, two-storied. There are children there, but there is no reason why any of them should have been in his back yard, leaving a naked doll on the ground.

Adventures of a Young Man

He awoke in the dark in the earliest hours of the third day in a cheap hotel room to see standing at the foot of his bed the faint image of a young woman in a blue hooded cloak. She said, "Come, follow me; it is time." She turned and walked toward the door, and he arose, already dressed, and followed her out the door, leaving the door open and nothing behind him.

He followed her down the hallway, a narrow passage with yellow walls and a thin carpet of uncertain gray to brown, lighted at each end by a bare bulb hanging by a strand of electrical cord. Standing at one doorway with a hand on the knob was a man in red, at another a man in yellow, at a third a man in white; none of them looked at him as he passed, just stared at the floor as if trying to recall something.

He followed the woman down the stairway at the end of the hall, winding down three floors, out into the lobby and past the desk clerk, who was asleep in his chair behind an iron grill, out onto the dark street, where she turned to the right and proceeded down the sidewalk.

The street was deserted, except for the three men: the man in red stood beneath a lamppost with his head and shoulders slightly bowed and his arms extended and hands apart as if holding a large package; the man in yellow stood at attention in the intersection ahead; the man in white stood inside the entryway of a shop that dealt in curios from small and poor South American nations—blowguns; shrunken heads of Guaraní children; small refrigerators with missing doors; dresses worn by female impersonators who had performed in mediocre tourist hotels; a piece of damp, dark cloth with a slightly sour smell. (He had seen all of this numerous times when he visited the store in his childhood; once with his father; several times, he thought, with his mother and her sisters. He had been in the store once at a time when it sold supplies and paraphernalia for spiritist rituals: table after table loaded with dusty tangles of herbs and grasses; candles; bottles of powdered viscera of bats and coral snakes; complete human skins stripped in the twinkling of an eye from unsuspecting office workers as they waited at bus stops and elevators; Haitian cigarettes in tin boxes; a profusion of small baskets and boxes woven of various natural fibers; small objects that he saw out of the corners of his eyes but was unable to bring into focus sufficiently long to identify them; and wild violets, jeweled with dew, pressing up everywhere through the endless piles of merchandise. Once, inside the shop, as he stood among the tables, he became vaguely anxious, fearful of being recognized as an enemy, and, looking about for a place to hide, he spied a large object of red glass and slipped behind it. As he looked through the thin and quite transparent glass, he gradually realized that this was a sculpture of a vulva, and he was standing within the curve of the concave side.)

Then the young man and his guide turned a corner and were standing before an immense and ancient mansion, which he had never before noticed but which he recognized had been there long before the city that surrounded it had been conceived. It was many stories high, though he didn't count. There were turrets and battlements and ledges, and windows of the deepest black; gargoyles and the Green Man everywhere; cornucopias spilling fruits and sheaves of grain; and carved along the faces of the ledges runes and glyphs and formulae and outlines of continents and scenes of love and hunting and battle. It was all in wine-red brick, in some places crumbling to dust that floated out onto the night air and fell slowly and silently toward the street: immensity and darkness looming against the stars; hovering doves; the possibility of a great forest within. The air bled.

The mansion was surrounded by a stone wall surmounted by a spiked iron fence. They stood before a gate that curved high above them, and the woman said, "This is the house of which you have been told. You have choices, which are both few and many. Find the box containing the Urim and Thummim, and hope that you will remember their use. Take this ring, on which you see carved in bdellium the last letter of the alphabet of the angels. Now, go."

He climbed seventy steps to the door. Upon entering, he found himself in a large foyer, the floor of which was cluttered with various computer-like machines and instruments, which he recognized as belonging to a French organization for the study of paranormal phenomena. To his right was another door into what appeared to be a receptionist's room. Behind the receptionist's desk sat a young man, Somalian, he thought, of urbane demeanor. He approached the young man and stood before his desk. The man looked up and said: "Good morning, sir. I will be with you momentarily."

He punched two keys on his computer, adjusted a thin stack of papers, and returned his attention to his visitor.

"How may I help you, sir?"

Without speaking, the visitor held the ring out to him. He took it, examined it, and said, "I see. Well."

The receptionist handed back the ring and sat back in his chair and folded his hands on his desktop.

"We have been waiting for you for some time. Some of us were beginning to lose hope. Are you ready?"

"I suppose so. There was nowhere else to go."

"What instructions have you received?"

"'This is the house of which you have been told. You have choices, which are both few and many. Find the box containing the Urim and Thummim, and hope that you will remember their use. Take this ring, on which you see carved in bdellium the last letter of the alphabet of the angels. Now, go.'"

"That's not much to go on, is it?"

"No, I suppose not.

"Well, let me show you to the entrance. Whether you go on or not is, of course, up to you, though we do have our reasons for hoping you will."

The receptionist arose and took the visitor back out to the foyer. At the rear of the foyer was a doorway the visitor hadn't noticed when he first came in. The casing was plain and white, like that of a bedroom or a closet of an ordinary house. The door itself was missing, though the brass hinges were still in place. An unlighted staircase rose from just within the door. The steps were of bare wood, and worn.

"We haven't picked up any movement here for several months. That's all I can tell you."

The visitor stood in the doorway and looked up the stairs. They disappeared into complete darkness about twenty steps up.

"All right," he said. "Thank you."

He climbed for a long time in the darkness. For a time he could see the bright rectangle of the door below when he looked back, but then it disappeared. He supposed the stairway had turned slightly in one direction or the other, though he hadn't noticed which.

He came to what seemed to be a landing. Feeling about, he found a door knob and turned it. The door opened inward into a hallway. He stepped inside and shut the door behind him.

He followed the hallway until it turned to the right, and he was standing inside a simple bedroom. A young woman—sandy-colored hair, a light gray sweatshirt, blue denim jeans—was making the bed. She flipped out the white sheet, let it settle, then worked around the bed tucking the edges under the mattress. She made hospital corners. She laid out the second sheet and tucked it under and made hospital corners at the foot. She laid out a quilt and a spread, folded them back, put pillows in place, and then tucked the bedding around them.

"The children are outside," she said. "I will call them for lunch in a few minutes."

She left the room, and he followed her.

The house was small. There was a small hallway from which two bedrooms and a bathroom opened. The hallway opened into a living room, which was spacious for the size of the house. One door of the room opened directly outside; the other into the kitchen. This was a wooden frame house. The floors were wood, and the varnish had mostly worn off. The living room floor was partially covered by a large worn rug of the same material as the carpet in the hallway of the hotel.

The kitchen door stood open. It was a warm, sunny day. There was a screen door, and he stood at the kitchen door looking out through the screen. There was a yard with grass, a high wooden fence around the yard, big leafy trees outside the fence all around the yard. There were blue sky and white clouds, the sound of bees, the drone of an airplane, the sound of hammering.

The woman opened the refrigerator and took out a glass bottle of milk and a package of baloney. She set them on the counter. She took a loaf of Wonder Bread in its white wrapper with red, blue, and yellow polka dots from a bread box and set it on the counter. She made a baloney sandwich and cut it in half and put the halves on separate plates. She made a peanut butter and blackberry jam sandwich and cut it and put the halves on the plates. She put a few potato chips on each plate. She poured milk into two glasses. She set everything on the table, a Formica table with chromed legs and vinyl and chrome chairs.

He was standing on the grass near the fence when she called the children. There was a smell of hot wood, the children frozen in the motions of going into the house, a bird frozen in the air just above the fence. A miniature of the glass vulva rested on a white embroidered cloth on the chest of drawers. A drawer slid open. As he reached out to touch the denim over her knee, she lay back, a mound of yellow sweet-smelling flowers in the sun, as one wall of the bedroom was no longer there. Always, it had been like this. He walked away with a pang of disappointment to look for the second door, down the long hallway, past the man in red (where were the yellow and the white?), back into the stairwell, groping about in the darkness, finding the stairs upward, climbing again into the darkness.

The second door. Another hallway, along each side stalls from which, as he passed, men and women performing a variety of erotic acts, most of which he thought he would not have enjoyed but some of which intrigued him, looked up at him with hostile eyes. He came to one stall that, unlike the others, was hidden by a partition. In the partition was a door on which was painted in black the last letter of the alphabet of the angels. He opened the door and found the stall empty, except for a high four-legged stool on which sat an ornately carved cedar box. He opened the box and found within it two crystal spheres the size of large marbles. He picked them up and examined them. He could not remember their use. He replaced them in the box and set the box on the stool and turned his attention to the walls of the stall.

They were completely covered with pictures of varying sizes. The largest were about the size of his hand, the smallest the size of the nail of one of his little fingers. He focused on one chosen at random. There was the girl in the blue cloak standing at a table in the spiritist shop holding in her hand and closely examining a two-pronged object that he couldn't make out, though it looked similar to the one he remembered having seen in the curio shop. He turned to another and saw the man in yellow holding a bunch of blue flowers resembling the wild violets he had seen growing in the curio shop. In another he saw the sandy-haired woman from the first door walking the hallway that led from the door into her house. The picture caught her midstep. Her back was to him, and in the foreground of the picture was a large, dark figure that seemed to be following her.

The figure's back also was turned to him, and he could not make out whether it was human or something else. Hanging from a nail on one wall of the hallway, somewhat ahead of the woman, was what appeared to be a white garment, and, just beyond the garment, a door. How had he overlooked that door before? On the door was the numeral 3 in brass. He would have to retrace his steps.

He turned to where the door of the stall had been, and it was no longer there. He looked all about him. There was no door anywhere. He also noticed then that there seemed to be no source of light in the room, yet he could see with perfect clarity. He found the picture of the girl in the blue cloak standing in the spiritist shop, but she had moved. She had turned away from the table, and her hand was reaching behind her to replace the two-pronged object. In the distance, unnoticed by the girl, the man in red, the man in yellow, and the man in white stood together, looking toward her. One of them held before himself a picture frame about two feet square, and within the frame, in black on a white background, was a single glyph: the last letter of the alphabet of the angels.

There were the letter, the ring, the two crystal spheres in the cedar box. Where was the door?

He reached into the picture and took hold of the letter with both hands, gripping it like the steering wheel of a cream-colored De Soto he once had driven down a country road in summer under a canopy of great leafy trees. He had been just previously lying in a field beyond the trees in a bed of yellow flowers, their heavy perfume rising like steam under the steady sun. What was her name? *Legion,* he was sure. He grasped the letter with both hands, but it refused to move. He let it go and returned to the cedar box. He opened it, removed the crystal spheres, and held them to his eyes. The receptionist sat before him behind his counter.

"Congratulations, sir," the receptionist said. "I see you are beginning to recall their use. Your choices have been many, but you have recognized few of them. This is the common experience of men. Her name was Legion, as you remembered. But fear not; I am with you always."

The vision closed, and he was alone again in the stall. He returned the spheres to the box and put the box in a pocket of his jacket. He went to the wall through which he had entered, thrust his hands into it, and tore it. He stepped through into the hallway and walked back in the direction from which he had come. The hostile inhabitants of the stalls were gone now, and scraps of yellowed newspaper blew in the wind across darkened streets. He went back through the second door and felt his way down the stairs to the first and went back through it. He brushed past the dark, hulking figure without discerning its identity, past the sandy-haired woman who was frozen midstep, past the white garment hanging from the nail, to the door to which was riveted the brass figure of the numeral 3, opened the door, and went through.

He was standing in a field of grass under a summer sun. The air was warm. At a short distance were the man in red, the man in yellow, the man in white; the first standing erect and looking toward the sun, the second crouching as if to kneel, the third on his knees with his face in his hands. To the right of them was the girl in the blue cloak, holding the two-pronged object in her hands with her head bowed, as if presenting it as an offering to a sacred image. To the right of her, the receptionist sat behind his desk, absorbed in a sheaf of papers. To the right of him the woman whose name was Legion stood on a mound of yellow flowers. Her jeans were cut away to expose her privates, and two holes were cut in her sweatshirt to expose her breasts. Behind him, he knew without looking, was the road that passed under the canopy of trees, and the cream-colored DeSoto moving along the road.

"Now we are making progress," he said aloud. He walked up to each of the figures in turn. Each was made of cardboard, supported by a flimsy wooden frame. They reminded him of a dream he had had as child, of giraffes standing about on a hillside, each made of cardboard supported by a wooden frame. He pushed each figure over in turn with a touch of his hand. They lay in the grass in the sunshine, and he stood with his hands clasped behind his back, gazing across the prairie, waiting for the last letter of the alphabet of the angels to appear over the horizon.

A Tale of Detection

i

The call from my partner, Dobson, comes shortly after midnight.

"I don't want to spoil the surprise," Dobson says. "You gotta see this for yourself."

It's in a lower middle-class neighborhood, nice houses, nothing special. This house is white, two stories, old. The crime scene is set up when I get there—flashing lights, yellow tape, uniforms all over the place. Dobson stands on the front porch.

"What's happening?" I ask him.

He shakes his head. "Nothing like I've ever seen," he says, "and I thought I'd seen it all."

I follow him through the front door. He touches the shoulder of one of the two uniforms who are standing in front of us, and they make way, and there's Mrs. Brineholt sitting on the living room sofa in red pants and top, rocking back and forth, holding the baby's head to her chest. Just the head. The body is nowhere in sight.

"Jesus, Mary, and Joseph," I say. "What is this?"

Dobson shakes his head again. "As far as we can figure out, they came home from a movie about eleven-thirty. The babysitter was gone, and the baby's head was sitting on the coffee table. We haven't found the body. A neighbor heard the screaming and called nine-one-one. By the time the first car got here, she was sitting like this, in shock. She won't let us take it away from her, and she won't communicate. There's an ambulance and a shrink on the way. We haven't found the babysitter, either."

"Where's the husband?"

"In the kitchen, looking pretty much like her. There's a uniform with him, too. Come on upstairs. You need to see the baby's room."

I follow him up the stairs.

The room is all pastel pink and yellow and white and blue, very clean and tidy, except for the crib and the floor around it. Evidently the baby was killed in the crib. The blankets are soaked with dark, clotted blood. It has puddled on the plastic mattress cover underneath and trickled down the side at one corner onto the floor.

"The killer must have put the body in some kind of a container, maybe a plastic bag, before he left the crib, because there's not a trace of blood anywhere else in the house. Must have put the head in a bag, too, to take it downstairs."

We go back downstairs. The lab boys are dusting for prints, cameras are flashing, the ambulance has arrived, and the shrink with a hypodermic needle to sedate the Brineholts, who are carried out on stretchers. The medical examiner puts the head in a plastic bag and puts that in a brown paper bag and takes it to the morgue. I give orders for armed guards to be put on the front and back doors twenty-four hours a day until further notice and go home to bed for four more hours.

Morning, Dobson and I are both at the precinct early. He's there first. I pull up a chair close to his desk and say, "Show me what we've got." He takes from a drawer of his desk a brown paper bag much like the one the medical examiner used a few hours ago, which he sets carefully on the desk top. The top of the bag is rolled. He unrolls it deliberately, then reaches inside and takes out and sets on the desk—at this point, memory fails me—either three highly polished silver balls the size of large marbles, or one grossly pornographic postcard addressed "To whom it may concern."

ii

In the darkness just before dawn a young woman carrying a white plastic trash bag loaded with a heavy, bulky object approaches a gate in a wall. The wall is made of cinder blocks and is more than eight feet high. The gate is of iron. It has no handle on the outside, only a small square hole covered on the inside. The young woman approaches the gate across a deserted street, looking nervously from side to side.

The gate is set inside the wall about two feet, and the entryway thus formed is darkly shadowed. The young woman steps into the darkness and raps three times on the gate with a small mallet she finds hanging there. The grated window opens immediately and a stern voice says, "What do you want?" The face behind the grating is invisible in the darkness.

"I'm the babysitter," the young woman whispers. "I've come to deliver the package and get new instructions."

The window cover slams shut with a metallic clink, and the gate begins to open inward, slowly and silently.

The young woman stands holding the white bag at her left side. She is very patient. Before the door has fully opened, the night, a day, and most of another night pass. Meanwhile, flowers from the gardens within the wall slip silently through the opening—hyacinth, iris, snapdragon, yellow daisy, orchid, tulip, daffodil, certain species of Campanula, the entire order Rubiales, one by one, like the notes of a lesser known étude of Chopin played very slowly, and join the procession passing on the street behind her.

This procession has its origin in a distant part of the city, where the players' costumes are manufactured in vile sweatshops situated at appropriate intervals on the banks of rivers, the confluence of which escapes the attention of most cartographers, however appreciative they might be of Chopin, of the craftsmanly murder of infants, of Rubiales, even of the more subtle varieties of alibi concocted by the most desperate criminals.

The procession passes this point on the street at almost the exact same time each morning, though sometimes later. The young woman knows nothing of this, of course, and only considers herself fortunate to witness so artful a display, which she watches by a kind of second sight without having to turn away from the gate. She remains in her place until the last wagon has passed, and her left leg becomes indistinguishable from those of the ivory statues on display in the quarters of the tailors who made the costumes, and the ivy creeps furtively up her inner thigh. The liberties taken by the ivy signal the moment for her to enter the garden.

iii

We conduct the interrogation on a tiled area near the fountain. We sit at a small table, the babysitter across from me, Dobson at my left. I place on the table a life-sized Latex model of the body of the infant as we imagine it must have looked in reality, while still intact.

"What do you know about this?" I ask.

"Who are you?" she asks. "Are you here to give me my new instructions?"

Dobson smirks. "Oh, we'll give you instructions, all right."

"What's in the bag?" I ask her, trying to ignore Dobson.

"I think I want to talk to an attorney," she says.

"Oh, we'll get you an attorney all right," Dobson says, continuing to smirk.

"If you won't give me new instructions, then I must show my attorney this," she says, pulling the hem of her dress far up on her left thigh. The leg is completely, thickly enveloped in ivy, almost to the top. My eyes are fixed on the two inches of snowy flesh between the edge of her dress and the top of the ivy. She extends the leg out to the side, until her heel rests several yards away in a patch of hyacinth that has failed to escape with its fellows.

I begin to fear that the case is insoluble, and I arise and walk slowly and sadly out to find the procession, leaving Dobson to his own devices.

I enter a small diner at noontime, not really expecting to find a seat open, but there is Dobson sitting at the counter with an empty seat at his left. Sitting on the counter in front of him, just beyond his plate, in fact, is the head, still showing not a sign of decomposition. I still marvel at how cleanly it has been cut off, so that it sits there on the stump of the neck as evenly and firmly as a bust of Pythagoras.

I haven't thought of Pythagoras in years.

I sit down beside Dobson.

"Well," I say, "any progress?"

"Plenty," he says. "You left too soon."

"Did she confess?"

"No. She's still holding out. But we expect her to crack any day now."

The head is beginning to undergo a transformation. It grows larger, and the angelic infant features are maturing, grossening. I order a toasted ham and cheese sandwich and watch the transformation progress while I wait. Dobson has already finished his lunch—a double cheeseburger with fries—and is drinking his coffee, holding the cup in two hands with his elbows resting on the counter, looking glumly down at the head. By this time it is that of a large, fat, and bald adult, rather resembling an older Mussolini.

"It keeps doing this," Dobson says. "Last time it was Charles Manson. The time before that it was some old Greek."

"Pythagoras," I say, instantly knowing.

"Yeah, him. How'd you know?"

I have no answer. I am lost in a memory of standing on a beach a long time ago, something like Miami Beach, looking at a lifeguard's tower, where the girl sits holding a baby, and ivy is growing up all about the tower, and from the tower in each direction along the beach as far as I can see is a line of busts of Pythagoras, carved in ivory, resting in the sand and looking toward the sea.

A New Job

"We'll start you in the Receiving Department."

I am truly grateful for the job.

"Take this paper through that door and give it to Sheryl. She'll tell you what to do."

I take the paper through the indicated door and find myself in an enormous open bay of desks where young men are working at computer terminals. Line upon line of desks, lines so long I can't see the end of them. Fluorescent lighting, beige and gray walls and floor, acoustical tile ceiling—your standard office, but so many desks.

A young woman sits at a counter to my right. I give her the paper and say, "I'm looking for Sheryl."

"Of course you are," she says, "and you should be truly grateful for the job."

She takes the paper and starts down the aisle between two lines of desks. She pauses to speak to someone, pauses as if to think, turns, pauses, continues on, working her way down the aisle, her dress a patch of blue here, there, moving down the aisle, becoming very small. Then I see that the far end of the office bay is a forest of pines. The blue patch moves into the forest and disappears among the trees.

Standing among the trees, sunlight filtering through the boughs and needles. Before me a building, like a warehouse, one story, concrete and steel, surrounded by a chain link fence with no gate in sight. Over the door a sign: "Receiving Department." The door opens inward, and a young woman steps out wearing blue denims, western boots, a white cotton shirt with the tails tied up to expose a lean abdomen. She leans against the wall to one side of the door with her right elbow resting in her left hand, holding a cigarette on which she draws from time to time. I standing watching her for a long time, wondering if this is Sheryl. All the time I watch her, the sun hardly seems to move.

"Come in," she says eventually, between draws on the cigarette.

There is still no way in, so I go to the right, along the fence line, which turns to my left. I follow the fence to the left for a while until I realize it extends beyond my sight into the forest. I stop and turn to look behind me and see it also extends out of sight the way I've just come. I wonder what to do. The sun is warm through the trees, the pines smell hot, and finally I am so overcome by sleepiness I lie down on the carpet of red, brittle pine needles and sleep.

In a hotel room, looking through the window toward a beach in late afternoon. The shadows are long. At the edge of the beach, silhouetted against the restless water, six giraffes are blazing furiously, great orange and yellow fires.

"I'm looking for...." and I stop, not knowing how to finish the sentence. I am speaking to a young woman who stands behind me, to my right. I can't see her, but it is impossible to be unaware of her presence.

"I know," she says, "but I can't help you without more information. So I suggest we stick to questions that can be answered, like 'how long can this go on?' "

The giraffes, who are all standing, writhe and contort, flinging up one leg, then another. Their mouths are open in silent screams. Indeed, how long?

A wind is up, and pennants flutter, blue and yellow. On each is embroidered in white block letters a word of which I can make out only "RY."

Waystation

A small house at the edge of a cliff overlooks a sea. The one door and all the windows have long since been removed by scavengers, but the scavengers are not vandals, and they have left undamaged the true treasure contained within this house: the pictures. The pictures cover the walls and ceilings; the door frames; the cupboards, inside and out; every inch of paintable surface is covered with them. There are undoubtedly many thousands of them, though no one is known to have counted. Some have begun but after several days have recognized the hopelessness of the task. One investigator found that some of the pictures moved to other locations even as he counted them. The pictures are of all sizes, some as large as the stretch of a man's arms and some so small that even with a magnifying glass one can barely make out the scenes depicted. The windows at the back of the house overlook the sea, and as seen through one of the windows the view is always sunlit, the sky always blue, the sea always blue and white-capped, no matter what the time of day or the weather or light conditions as seen from outside. At times the wind sweeps rain throughout the house, but the pictures are miraculously undamaged. The colors have never faded, and in some cases seem actually to have brightened with the passing of years. Once as I stood in the kitchen, looking out toward the sea, I was certain that a woman sat at the table behind me, drinking tea and turning the pages of a volume of verse, but I understood that if I turned she would not be there, so I continued looking out the window. The air was laden with a scent of mowed grass warming in summer sunlight. Later I found a picture of her, about as large as the palm of my hand, sitting at that very table with the very cup of tea and a book, but she was turned slightly away from me and I couldn't see her face. Beside that picture was another of a man walking along a road bordered on either side by a stone wall overgrown with a perfect profusion of roses. He wore a broad-brimmed hat of the kind seen in pictures of Goethe and carried a staff, and he appeared to be moving at a leisurely pace beneath the summer sun. I recognized that road; it passed a mere mile from the cliff's edge. So far as I know I have never met the man himself, although I have sometimes remembered that I myself was the man. I sometimes remember walking leisurely along that road, raising dust in the motionless air, knowing I was approaching the lane that turned toward the house. I don't remember having actually arrived at the house on that journey, and often I remember nothing of the journey at all.

There Were Several Reasons Why This Wouldn't Work

There were several reasons why this wouldn't work. For one, the road extended indefinitely beyond the horizon, down a narrow hallway papered in yellow and hung with the ivory arms of lost infants. For another, a mirror hung in the air in innumerable particles of glittering dust, remembering vaguely its old place on the wall of a small house in woods, or peering out from among the clotted roots of cedars and spruces. I have tried to explain this, but you know how it was: money was scarce, the weather uncertain, the smell of the spruces under the hot sun heavy in the air. Then the children came, a procession of them, so many, shuffling silently along the yellow corridor, eyes wide and soft and sad, thinking of earlier days when they conversed freely with deer whose antlers were bright with rain. We lay on our bed, propped on our elbows, watching them, hardly conscious of our nakedness, remembering light on ancient seas.

YELLOW SNAKES

A man was watching the movements of a yellow snake as thick as his wrist and as long as he was tall. He stood on a strip of broken, weed-grown asphalt, holding a baby cradled in his left arm, with his right hand supporting, the baby loosely wrapped in a pastel blue cotton blanket with a corner laid over his face to protect it from the sun. The heat was beginning to be oppressive. He smelled the asphalt, and the weeds were drooping.

Rising up from the old asphalt road was an embankment of granite stones the size of the baby's head, an embankment as massive as the face of a great dam. At the top of the embankment, out of sight, beyond the upper edge, was the highway. The baby's mother, who had been the man's wife, was waiting there, sitting on the shoulder of the highway with her back against the protective barrier. Her back was turned to him; he knew that.

He knew that this country had no venomous snakes; he had heard that; all of his life he had believed that; he remembered that; and he thought of it as he watched the sinuous tube of yellow emerge from the stones a few yards up the embankment and disappear again among stones a few yards away. There must be mice living under the stones, he thought. He felt the heat around him rise by degrees. If he did not begin climbing the embankment right away, he would need to find shade, and there was some below the asphalt road, under the trees that grew along a trickle of creek. He could rest there for a while.

But he did not. He began to pick his way carefully up the stony slope. The tips of thistle leaves emerged tentatively between stones ahead of him. Where there are thistles there may be the yellow snakes, he remembered. He picked his way carefully. The baby beside him held the little finger of his left hand and tried to keep up, but the man knew that it was difficult for him. The asphalt road behind him was becoming crowded with trailer trucks, the great blue boxes rattling their sides together, and he wondered if the woman would wait for him. A snake leaped from between two stones toward his face and he batted it away with his right hand, startled.

He remembered the first time he had seen one of these yellow snakes. It was a long time ago, when he was a boy.

How had he come to be at the bottom of this embankment, standing alongside this broken piece of the old, two-lane highway? He did not remember, though he supposed that he must have come over the hills behind him. He had come from somewhere beyond those hills. A fragmentary memory came to him of carrying the infant through a tangle of tall grass, in the heat of an early August afternoon, watching large yellow snakes as thick as his own thigh squirm slowly away from his steps, his careful, slow steps.

He turned to his left to find his former wife standing beside him, knowing that she simultaneously was sitting with her back against the protective barrier above him, and he said to her, "I'll try to get to you in time. I'll try to get to you before they come. Please wait for me."

"I'll be there," she replied. "There is still time."

And then he was alone. He wondered if it would be easier to drop down across the road and into the ravine. He did so, and standing in the creek in the bottom of the ravine he grasped at a fish with both hands, but it slipped away into the reeds; and he looked back up the slope to the highway above, and the woman, now with his own face, and a yellow snake coiled on her lap, looked up and said, "I will wait. There is still time."

ON A THURSDAY

I last saw her in the middle of an afternoon in late June, unseasonably cool, and I was eating a sandwich at a food court in a shopping mall. It was a Thursday. I was alone at a table by a wall, and I saw her walking quickly along the opposite side. She was wearing a white dress printed with small red flowers, also wearing a pale blue sweater and carrying a white purse hanging from her left shoulder. Her hair was cut shorter than usual, but still blonde, held back from her ears by red barrettes. It flounced a bit as she walked, quickly, intently, looking directly forward, not turning her head, and she didn't see me.

The instant I saw her I put down my sandwich and went after her. I called her name, but she seemed to pay no attention, just kept walking. I dodged between the tables as politely as I could, but I couldn't reach her before she turned the corner into the mall concourse. I turned after her and walked fast, careful not to bump into people but hurrying. She kept walking, and I kept following, but I couldn't catch her. She exited the mall by the south exit and continued down the sidewalk. I kept following, but I couldn't seem to move fast enough. We walked on and on, out of the city center, into a rundown section of pawnshops and sandwich counters and adult bookstores and parking garages, then car lots and a Blue Boutique, the Southern Xposure Club for Members Only, then more car lots. We came to where weeds grew up through cracks in the sidewalk, then a vacant lot, then warehouses and wholesale dealers. I was nearly a block behind her when she suddenly cut across the street—a deserted street—and went through the door of a large, high, windowless and nameless building. I followed her across and through the door, and I was in a large open bay filled with desks and computer terminals and keyboard operators. The ceiling was high, and the bay was lighted by bright fluorescent lamps. She walked down an aisle between desks, and I followed behind, and she went through a door at the back of the room, and I followed, and as I passed through the door I saw as in a vision the immensity of the place, buildings and parking lots and more buildings, and she was out there somewhere, and I walked on frantically, desiring to smell her perfume on that blue sweater and feel its softness against my face again.

BANNERS OF PAST LIVES

We departed early, raising banners of past lives before us. The road lay through a run-down subdivision on the edge of the city, a place where housewives still hung clothes on lines to dry. One wore a dark blue dress with a low hem and long sleeves, and a light-blue bandanna around her head and a white apron. She kept the clothespins in a large pocket on the apron. Her husband, who had lost an arm in combat, sat inside in the breakfast nook reading a newspaper and drinking lukewarm coffee. It was necessary for him to lay down the paper each time he wanted to pick up his cup. They still made love, however, usually in the woman-astride position, though occasionally in the "crayfish." When he heard the commotion raised by our passing, the husband came to the doorway to watch, wearing the expression of a man remembering a past life, a life of gallantry and glory in long-past wars, in that southern country where the housewives are often trapped in the walls, moving about silently in the dark spaces .

We were tired. The previous night we had ascended and descended stairways endlessly, remaining resolutely cheerful, but tired. We always were tempted to open one of the doors that we occasionally passed on the stairways, hoping to find a comfortable place to lie down, but rest came rarely to us it was necessary to keep moving as long as possible, though there was no definite requirement, only a sense of inescapable duty. We therefore departed early, raising the banners of past lives.

At a rest stop, we sat at picnic tables in the shade of cottonwood trees and watched the travelers stroll on the grass and consider their plans. The place was infested with snakes, mottled red snakes about twelve inches long. They were being called "coral snakes," though I knew that was incorrect. They had short, needle-sharp teeth and the ability to leap into the air fully extended, the tip of the tail attaining to one or two inches above the ground. They caused much apprehension, but there was reason to believe that they were not venomous. A young man whom I knew to be somewhat impulsive in his behavior was playing with one of them, teasing it, pulling at its tail, holding it and shifting it from hand to hand. "I hope you will let that go," I said to him, and he replied, "I want to do this." The previous night, I had passed him on the stairs, and it had occurred to me then that he might be troublesome.

HOMECOMING

I recall a large hole excavated through the asphalt of a street; a yellow inflatable raft imbedded in the gravelly earth of one side of it; for some reason the road workers had left it exposed. We had buried that raft there two years before because it had a leak we couldn't patch and the city hadn't yet supplied us with trash barrels, then the street had been put through and our secret covered over by asphalt. Before coming upon it, I had found it necessary to ascend through a flowing creek that spread out over a slope, ankle deep in water. I could have stepped to the side into shallower water, but it was swifter there, over larger and possibly slippery gravel, and even with my walking stick I preferred to avoid the risk. At the top of the slope was a large patch of grass and weeds, then a wood fence with a gap, and beyond the gap I found myself back in the subdivision. That was where I came on the hole in the asphalt, with the inflatable raft, near our house. But I have neglected to mention the snakes. Lying at the top of the slope was a four-foot section of tree trunk, perhaps a foot in diameter, weathered smooth and gray. As I put one foot over it, I saw a snake stretched out on the ground just in front of me, patterned like a rattlesnake, a good three feet long, but no thicker than my index finger, with a narrow head, immediately identifying it as nonvenomous, but it was bad tempered, striking out at my walking stick. I fended it off with the stick, and it slipped under the log and went on its way. Then another snake emerged suddenly from a hole in the ground, this one considerable thicker, perhaps two inches, black with yellow and red rings. I immediately thought "coral snake," but the coloring was wrong. What struck me about this specimen was what looked very much like blonde hair on its head, long enough to be combed back and parted. I allowed it to exit its hole and vanish into the weeds a few feet away. It was then that I passed through the weeds (taking care to probe ahead of me with my stick for the snake) and then through the gap in the fence into the subdivision, where a woman holding the second snake expected me.

September 2014

A Door Stands Open, beyond It the Sun

A door stands open, beyond it the sun; people walking in and out, through the door into the sun, from the sun through the door, figures in black silhouette; a door like any ordinary door in a house, a door with knobs. I am lying, half conscious, unable to feel my legs, on the bed with the iron stead that sits against a wall of the hallway where people pass, going and coming. An indistinct form appears beside the bed, a hand touches my head, and a voice as if coming from a great distance says, "Rise up, and walk," and I rise from the bed to walk with those who come from the sun, down a winding staircase to the street outside to mingle with the swirling throngs.

I try a shop door and it opens. A meeting is in progress—the seven members of the Disaster Preparedness Committee sit around a U-shaped conference table, three members on each arm of the U facing each other, the chairman sitting at the bottom of the U facing the door that I have just opened. I stand, uncertain what to do. The chairman looks up at me, and then all the other members turn to look.

"Please take a seat," the chairman says, and I take a chair against the wall to one side. It occurs to me that I have some responsibility connected with this committee. A strange feeling comes over me, with the shadow of a memory—I have been here before.

I have difficulty following the discussion, my mind wanders, and I catch only a few words and phrases: "imminent," "utmost urgency," "possibly beyond our resources," "the bridge," "burial teams."

Then the chairman turns to me again and asks, "Does all of this meet with your approval? Do you have any further directions for us?"

I am surprised, but I sense that the safest answer for me to give is, "Yes, yes, of course. Keep me informed. I will issue new directives as necessary."

That seems to satisfy the committee members, and they all stand and disperse, leaving me alone in my chair. I envision the ground quaking outside and fissures opening to reveal multicolored strata of earth and rock and in the depth of the largest fissure the white light of the sun.

December 2014

Trail Descends and Narrows

Trail descends and narrows
Not like this on the ascent
Rock face on right
Deep water on left
Rock face overhanging trail
Impossible to pass upright
It has changed
Easier on the ascent
Leaning backward over water
Clinging to rocks
Stepping sideways
Uncertain handholds
On quartz and granite
Crumbling
Overhang of rock face sharpens
Trail narrows
Hanging backward over water
Over chasm
Would be worse with pack
Safe ground and trees
Just beyond crumbling rock

September 2014

A Sphere Grows inside My Breast

A sphere grows inside my breast
Green and smooth
It begins quite small, steadily enlarges
Until it no longer fits inside my body
I do not feel it, there is no pressure
The spreading surface passes through my organs and beyond my skin
Painlessly, silently
I would not notice it did I not see it in the vision of the mind
Is this a bad thing, or a good thing?
Is there cause for alarm?
How far will it go?
Beyond my house?
Beyond the earth?
Beyond the solar system and outward?
It reminds me of spheres I remember in paintings by Magritte
Resting on the ground among houses, as large as houses
People go about their business as if the spheres were not there
Perhaps it is better to ignore them
Their existence poses unsettling questions
As the sphere continues to grow
I will go fishing
To a small lake in woods
Hidden among dark firs
I will fish with artificial flies
Cast out among lily pads
The water lilies are in bloom, yellow

November 2014

Looking Down a Narrow Valley

Looking down a narrow valley where a river runs straight
Both sides heavily wooded with fir and spruce
A notch of clear sky in the distance where the river drops over the
 horizon
Hanging in the notch against the blue sky
An enormous boulder of weathered limestone
Carved with letters of a language I do not know
They are scripture of a vanished race
I touch the carvings with my finger tips
Tiny grooves
A long step from the top of the boulder to the left ridge of the canyon
But the air among the trees is sweet
The odor of fir and spruce needles warmed by the sun
The vision of the unknown alphabet is clear in the memory
As I sit cross-legged in the mouth of a cave
Behind me in hooded robes, some of blue and some of red
Are the members of a band of itinerant scholars
Or perhaps they are workmen, or jugglers
They are very small

Letters of the unknown alphabet scratched into the walls of the cave
On the ceiling and the walls
And a drawing of an unknown animal
An animal with long legs and a hornless head
It speaks slowly but its words cannot be made out
The girls who attend it are gowned in diaphanous gauze
That would catch fire if exposed to the sun
One of them points at letters on the wall

And gazes back expectantly, as if waiting for a response
But in the distance the river flashing in code demands attention

The small men in red and blue are dispersed among the trees
Birches have grown up among the firs
Smooth pebbles exude from small holes in the bark
And slide in orderly streams down the trunks
Pebbles red and blue
A letter carved on each of them

The boulder fragments as if from within
The pieces move apart slowly
Blue sky appears between them
They cease to move
The cluster holds its position
The girls approach from behind
Careful to remain in shade

The key to the unknown language is kept in a box
At the back of the cave
One of the girls sits on it
The other moves a finger on the wall, writing

November 2014

Pregnant Moving Vans Jostle Together on the Highway

Pregnant moving vans jostle together on the highway
The flowing hair of the lead truck sinks into the summer sun like
    fishing line
The bread falling in cubes from the power lines overhead
Assembles itself into braided ropes
They strangle the doves of minimal efficiency
That carpet the pavement in slow imitation of musical chairs
Meanwhile the very thin wife of the local police chief
Bares her wrists to display in a shop window
The blue tattoos of an atrophied love

November 2014

THE DOVES OF MINIMAL EFFICIENCY

The doves of minimal efficiency cling tenaciously to their ancient
 privileges
Inking their maps on the walls of abandoned police stations
Composing music under the shelter of desert camouflage
Storing their eyes at night in small cedar boxes
When not observing through slits in the ceilings the movement of
 armies
Through the warehouses where lost battles are stored

November 2014

The Apex of an Isosceles Triangle

The apex of an isosceles triangle etched behind the cornea of a carp's
    eye
Trembles like a severed lip cowering in the interstice of a moth's
    wing and A flat
While the sun sleeps untroubled between the breasts of the
    Shulamite
With a pre-dynastic king-list carved in bas-relief below her navel
Apple blossoms erupt from all the hair of her body

September 2014

Fishhooks Tied to Silken Filaments

Fishhooks tied to silken filaments
Trail behind words like dogs circling to make their beds
Or the odor of dreams
Dragged through streets after rain
Such are the ruminations of the tenured philosophers
Who stroll among photographs of aging porn stars
Talking of spider webs that drift across the corpses of unicorns and
    poets
The subtle modeling of which illustrates eons of hope and hesitation

September 2014

Walking in the Shadow of the Sun's Memory

Walking in the shadow of the sun's memory
I pause to brush away the leaves from inside my face
The notes of last night's concerto swollen with rage
Crashing against a cliff's face
Exploding brains of bison
That lately wandered the streets of a deserted city
The brains exude the odor of a woman's breath

September 2014

The Delicate Music of the Spheres

The delicate music of the spheres that grow in the breasts of street
    magicians
Conjures wars out of a thin line of memory
As the mathematics of lunacy leaks from the moon's fear
And fills the air with groans of dying strategy
The wars emit a music of their own
That inspires gangs of urchins who drag boats through empty
    boulevards
And run their fingers along the corner line of every wall and ceiling
Seeking a path to the sea

20 January 2015

THE INDECISION OF A LARK'S TONGUE

The indecision of a lark's tongue
Licking the inner thigh of a weeping statue
The statues weep throughout the city for the children lost
Wandering the plain through misted blood

September 2014

Dawn Breaks Crimson from the Music Box

Dawn breaks crimson from the music box
Its color tinges the face
Of the woman of papier mâché hands who looks out the window
The border of her robe drapes the floor and the furniture
The robe of forest-green velvet
Its hem is a chain of glass cubes
They have been dragged through the shimmer of kisses
That spreads across the valley below the window
When you kiss her her lips are wooden bannisters
Of stairways in hunting lodges where Blue Beard composes music
The music box plays one of his lullabies
When you touch the woman's hand it breaks off
Fragments of paper float up from the stub
They are engraved with secrets in cypher even she does not know
She begins to sing
Her song is a guillotine blade
That divides the kisses evenly among her lovers

November 2014

A Dream Wrapped in Rain Wrapped in a Dream

A dream wrapped in rain wrapped in a dream
Stands naked shivering outside the shrine
Contemplates the procession through the night
Of white and red and cobalt blue
And writes equations on falling snow

September 2014

THE DAY ARRIVES LATE

The day arrives late
Disheveled as having hastily left a lover
Her gown unhooked absentmindedly
To reveal between her shoulder blades
A window facing on a neglected garden
Where burnt corpses of invading metaphysicians provide cover for
    children
To play hide-and-seek with the queen's chief torturer
Who secretly conspires with the hovering dust raised by vanished
    horsemen
To tattoo inside her right thigh an image of her left thigh
The day regrets having left her lover

September 2014

The Tumescent Orchid That Lies Ignored on the Altar

The tumescent orchid that lies ignored on the altar
Recalls a time past
When legs of brittle newspaper
Supported a bedspring between the gate pillars of the temple
That was before the packs of coyotes with the hide torn from their
    chests
Before the concubines of the high priest
And then the news of a train derailed in the remote Himalayas
Floating for one ecstatic moment
A spider's filament glinting sunlight
Before hurtling into an abyss of piano keys and velvet

September 2014

THE PIANO KEYS MELT SLOWLY
IN THE AFTERNOON SUN

The piano keys melt slowly in the afternoon sun, but inexorably,
Recalling the flow of spiced honey through long and white fingers
And onto the nylon-stockinged thighs of a dreaming poetess.
She picks raspberry seeds from between her teeth and plants them
    on the ivories,
Dropping them one by one into holes pried open by a darning
    needle in the hand of an armless mannequin.
I watch from under the wallpaper,
Taking care not to draw attention to myself.
The pistol in my right trouser pocket, however,
Sends forth green sprouts that become entangled in the works of all
    the clocks in the palace.
I urge it telepathically to be more discreet,
But it holds itself aloof from all direct interaction with human
    beings.
The poetess rouses herself from her languor to hover above the
    keyboard of the piano.
The keys are the petals of blossoming lies;
Her fingers flutter in them, attempting to coax out a note or two.

December 2014

A Thread of Light Floats

A thread of light floats in a darkened hallway
The walls poised and wary
Breath slow as the sap
In the lilacs growing from the roof

September 2014

Though I Feared We Might Find Happiness Together

Though I feared we might find happiness together
A convocation of wood lice absconded with the letters of our poem
Where now is the sunlight that escaped between the curtains of your
  face?
Where the white rabbits that frolicked on the small of your back?
One of your breasts was a fallow deer swimming against the current
  of the Nile
The other a locked room storing souvenir bus tokens from before
  the war
To think of you is to be trapped on a stairway between walls of fire
Hearing the distant performance of a Scarlatti mass
As a white rabbit descends the stairs
Trailing dreams of sunflowers

September 2014

I Keep Your Kisses in a Box

I keep your kisses in a box
I take them out to count them in the long evenings
When memories tiptoe furtively across the walls
I keep them in a paper box that once held chocolates wrapped in foil
Red and blue and gold and silver
The kisses rattle when I shake the box
They were not so small and hard when you gave them to me

December 2014

I Hide in the Deep Grass of My Heart

I hide in the deep grass of my heart
All the women I have loved are oval mirrors
Standing silent sentinel along the walls of a hallway
They will see me if I move
Their eyes are my nipples in turns through the long night
I must not look at them
An enemy moves silently along the hallway
Looking this way and that, rifle at the ready
I carefully part the grass with my hands
In a moment of inattention the enemy walks into one of the mirrors
But only part way, part of him remains outside the mirror
He seems to be trapped
The grass is water draining between my fingers

October 2014

THE TWISTED ROPE OF DAY

The twisted rope of day falls in a heap on the floor
I hide in a fetal position in the box that hides inside your ribs
Last night I opened the door of your left breast and removed a clock
The clock sits covered by a cape of swans' beaks on a chest of drawers
It hides from the wolf of cracked glass
That slithers about the room against the walls
I float backward through the wood of the box
Through your ribs
Through your skin
I stand naked on the window sill
I am the shadow of irresolution
I am the minute hand of the clock
Your kisses are snowflakes that swirl about me
When the river in which the swans bathe splits into three paths into
    the trees
The wolf of cracked glass removes the swans' beaks in the presence
    of strangers
Who come from the woods dragging their metaphysics behind them
Your kisses are whiter than wolf's teeth evanescing through the
    window
The door of a swan's breast opens inward
On a room where a woman transforms herself into a box of
    umbrellas
They are painted with scenes of last night's love
Your kisses are eyes watching from my skin
They are strangers lecturing on metaphysics

November 2014

Such Happiness Is Rare

Tangled filaments of memory
The intense wiring of a clear mind
Glitter in moonlight on the plain of remorse
A fox's teeth play musical chairs under the stars
Faces peer out from within walls
Then hide beneath a stair
Such happiness is rare

I will go, I will sing
With the merchants of string
Who roll on the floors through well lighted halls
Of ivy and swamp gas and exploding aeroplanes
Such happiness is rare

We will frolic on the plain thick with fleas
That lick the toes of Belgian burlesque dancers
To celebrate the night of the long knives
Protruding like grass from the bellies of wolves
The knives are very fragrant

I roll my nylon stockings down
They collapse with fatigue on quivering blueprints
Of structures of varnished wood and painted letters

I stand in a street in heavy traffic
In the heat of an August afternoon
Your breath is damp on my neck
Such happiness is rare

November 2014

As an Automobile Soars Off a Cliff's Edge

As an automobile soars off a cliff's edge
There is still time for the clown who is driving to adjust his makeup
The couple making out in the back seat look up surprised by the
    sudden rise in the pit of the stomach
"Carpe diem," one of them says and they go back to their business
Unknown to the occupants of the vehicle its launching over the cliff
    is the signal
For an army deployed in the valley below to begin its attack
As soon as the commanding general can remember the objective
The intelligence officer in charge of the sitmap has thought that he
    was playing Risk
As it turns out, the automobile makes a soft landing
After exiting the young man tucks a Risk board under his arm
And begins what he knows will be a long wearisome slog
Through miles of tangled underthings

October 2014

A Book of Lamentations

i

How doth the city sit solitary
—Lamentations 1:1

How doth the City sit solitary
One white arm thrust out of the broken plaza
Grasping toward the sky
Deserted temples surround the plaza
Darkness within their portals
Pillars white as the arm
The City lies spread behind the mind
The river spread out, dark water
Heads bobbing toward the sea
Deserted piers, warehouses, factories along the riverbanks
Small shops where masks once were made
For processions of acrobats and soothsayers
Dancing through the boulevards
To the unrestrained songs of murdered dogs
While copulating in the shadow of the shrine
Couples as ardent as butterflies' wing dust
Left the imprints of their bodies on the dissolving marble
And where is the girl who opened the cupboard below her breasts
To let spill the glyphs of Abraham's last Apocalypse?
An unidentified finger tracing one by one
The bones of her spine and the knobs of the cupboard doors
To lie with her the empty robe of the high priest
Would sacrifice one by one

The threads of which the soothsayer by the river wove it
And therein is the reason why the soothsayer's liver is poured upon
    the earth
His grief greater than that of a cedar tree bereft of its bones
As it reaches futilely for the hand through the veil
And the head of the king
Scraps of yellowed newspaper sewed to his tongue
Grins through the shattered windshield of a decaying automobile
At rest in the dry grass that grows between the legs of a broken statue
Of the girl who lost the glyphs
The king and the soothsayer yearn to be obeyed again
By the refugees scattered across the plain
Who hang their cooking pots on tripods constructed of discarded
    windshield wipers
And think of the faces that saw through the veil
The wedding ceremony of the girl who lost the glyphs

September 2014

ii

*How hath the Lord cast down the daughter of Zion with a cloud in his anger,
and cast down from heaven unto the earth the beauty of Israel
—Lamentations 2:1*

Cast down from heaven into the earth
The City is unrecognizable to the legless children who float above
    the streets
Between the dark-windowed skyscrapers of the previous age
Searching for lost memories that hide
Somewhere heaped up like discarded fast-food containers
They lost their legs in encounters with discredited theories
That fell one by one from the last rainbow

That was before the sea rolling over in its sleep like a post-coital angel
Flooded the earth with rationalizations

October 2014

iii

Behold in this horn were eyes like the eyes of man, and a mouth speaking
great things
—Daniel 7:8

The horn half buried in a patch of dandelions
Proliferating on the ceiling of the king's apartment
Has the eyes of a man and a mouth speaking great things
Its eyes look down upon the king
Who leafs through the pages of a coffee table book
A compilation of illustrated reports of the steady encroachment on
    his kingdom
By the floating hoards of legless children
He especially likes the pictures painted in the manner of Utrillo's
    early watercolors
He shows one to his favorite concubine
Who sits beside him sorting buttons in the dresser drawers that are
    her eyes
Red ones to the left, yellow ones to the right
Occasionally a few words incomprehensible to the king issue from
    the mouth of the horn
The concubine especially likes the buttons that are the color of the
    dandelions

October 2014

iv

Better is the sight of the eyes than the wandering of the desire
—Ecclesiastes 6:9

Better is the sight of the eyes
Than tents of grass erected on the soft flesh of the moon
They burst into flame at the merest touch of a coyote's breath
The eyes ask little of the moon
Though the daily labor of sweeping the corners of a coyote's den
With a fan of earrings
Becomes tedious in the early hours
When a fingernail inscribing small circles on a lover's hip
Drifts into fitful sleep
It dreams of a hallway that opens onto a busy street
Flashing windshields grit blowing in hot wind right turn only
     Mexican Grill I-90 1 Mile
1XU P41 will work for food green arrow coyote broken in the gutter

October 2014

v

Moreover the profit of the earth is for all: the king himself is served by the field
—Ecclesiastes 5:9

The king himself is served by the field
Of sequined lilies that spreads itself out on a sheet of graph paper
But he fades in and out with modulations of jazz guitar
The king finds this disconcerting
He takes consolation by resting his hand on a thigh of morning haze
Sheets of graph paper slip discreetly between the guitar notes
But the king snatches them out
Hides them under the hazy thigh

October 2014

And should not I spare Nineveh, that great city?
—*Jonah 4:11*

The serpent coiled beneath my diaphragm has passed a sleepless
    night
It looks restlessly this way and that
If I lie motionless it may slip away along the bones of my arm and
    out a fingertip
And so I lie on my back and watch the oval discs that drift about
    the room
They are the memories of lost loves and interrupted kisses
One rotates gracefully on its vertical axis and exits through an open
    window
I press myself backward against the underside and watch the land-
    scape slide away below
If the serpent departs here it will fall helplessly undulating
That would amuse me
On the upper side of the disc out of my sight is a forgotten cityscape
    of Monsù Desiderio
On the base of the principle monument is painted the face of the
    last queen
If you draw near she will insert her tongue into your mouth
And in gratitude permit you to caress with the tip of your own
    tongue
The inner surfaces of all her teeth
That prospect evokes a memory of a warm day in a flowering pear
    grove
I shall not speak of it
Meanwhile the discs in my room tire of their movement and rest
    themselves against a wall
Each an unsmiling portrait

My disc leans itself against the inner wall of the city
I step down from it to walk hand in hand with two members of the
   procession
That issues from within the half-melted mansion of Monsù's widow
She devotes her days to embroidering her legs with conjugations of
   obsolete verbs
I note that the city wall is built of the teeth of the last queen
Where against it is one permitted to press one's forehead to pray?

I sit in the shade of a vine on a hillside above the city
The serpent is coiled in the grass beside me finally asleep
But by a kind of telepathy we converse at length
He is of the opinion that the current regime has lost the mandate
   of heaven
And I incline to agree
But prefer to contemplate the hypothetical eruption in the ruined
   streets
Of pear blossoms in silent incessant convulsion

October 2014

Looking for the Captain

"Look," I say to a woman whom I love but who I am not sure loves me. "Look," I say. Mushroom clouds, small, indicating that they were at a great distance, are faintly visible in the black sky, just above the horizon. I look about us; people are milling, talking, arguing, gesticulating. No one else seems to notice the clouds. "When they notice, there will be chaos," I say. "We must find the captain." The captain is an officer deserving of respect. He is a man of good sense and the only one who might be able to keep order when the chaos threatens. The woman—a girl, really, a girl with shoulder-length hair and dressed modestly in a dress of white deerskin—nods in agreement, and we set out. We look first in the dining hall, but the captain is not there. We ask for him by name in the lounge, but no one has seen him. I watch the girl from the corner of my eye, but she does not look back. She is quite lovely, I think, and I wish she would take my hand. I notice the way the dress clings to the front of her body. We ascend the rocky face of a cliff and rest near the edge, but not for long. An automobile careens down the slope above us and explodes as it goes over the edge, the debris falling into the valley below. A second one does the same. We move away from the edge into a nearby patch of pines, hoping to find protection from the enemy automobiles, but there is little. A handsome young man whose wife is in the area says, "Are you with us? We need to move you on; it isn't safe here." He stands at the edge of the cliff with me, and we gaze together into the valley, at the bottom of which is dense tropical forest. "Most people enter the valley at one end or the other and don't get much further in," the young man says. "I prefer to explore the center. So does the captain." I stand looking down into the valley, wondering if the girl is near. I consider with a sense of some urgency the alternative routes into the center.

October 2014

LET THERE BE LIGHT

"Let there be light"
And there is darkness
(Lao Tzu knows about it)
It comes out of the forest
Through the trees
As uncertain
As faltering
As a broken-footed revolver
"Then let us go fishing," a man said
(The man in the Stetson hat)
"Let us paddle across the river in the summer sun"
Because the bridge is down
The bridge wraps itself around the legs of old women and young girls
Melting in the sun's heat
Like wax flowing from the wings of Icarus
The wax runs down a fire chute
And through the fingers
The sun rolls down the highway
A brass disk
Making a sound of embroidered violins
Grown from the calyx of a white orchid
Its thighs are clasped about your head
The old woman arrives carrying a lantern
The old woman who explains everything
If you put a coin over each of her eyes
She plays the piano on an iceberg like nobody's business
The old woman guards the explanations
She wraps her legs in castoff watercolors

To ward off the dreams that issue from her dried sex
Each dream is a fugitive shadow of hope
For the better times depicted in the discarded paintings
The bridge is down
The skyscrapers curl into themselves
They are crayons, melting
The cranes flying overhead
The five white cranes in a diamond formation
Transmit telepathic reports of distant wars
Working my way laboriously through the tangled girders of the
    bridge
I pick up crayons as I go
Windshields flash from the busy street across the river
Windshields decorated with decals of white cranes
A map of the former city is drawn between my beloved's breasts
    with a black crayon
We walk hand in hand through a corridor in a collapsing skyscraper
It is a corridor through the forest
The walls are green-leafed trees
Small snakes rest coiled on the branches
My lover's thighs are pressed together
A box of coiled wires rests in her pubic hair
The wires become a key
The old woman knows what it opens

December 2014

LINGERING OVER A PAGE OF GENESIS

Lingering over a page of Genesis
The author was dealing with other problems
Other flowers viewed through a wall by x-ray vision
Flowers with broad sword-like petals
Reminiscent of river banks where tall girls walk
Unstitching themselves slowly for lovers who watch from the rushes
Unstitching themselves with delicate movements
Pretending to be oblivious
Other times, other problems
Looking out the window with a finger marking the place:
"Let the waters be gathered together in the womb of the Queen
Of unstitched fingers scattered on the river bank"
Why has no one else ever noticed that line?

17 January 2015

Peel the Walls Away from the Brain

Peel the walls away from the brain
The brain an orange
The sections come apart in the hand
The woman standing in the brain scans the horizon for threatening
    ravens
A raven plucks a section from the brain, sucks out the juice
A traveler by the seashore thrusts a hand into the sun
Ravens billow from the wound
Followed by gouts of the sun's blood
Orange

The sun, the sun
Come from the sun, reach into the sun
Thrust a hand into the sun
Born inside the sun
Contain the sun
When the wall splits the sunlight bursts in
The sun contained within the rib cage leaks between the ribs
Lie down on the floor among scurrying small snakes
They do not like the sun
They lick the ribs
They do not like the taste

Paint a picture on the wall with the sun's blood
Orange

2 January 2015

Blue Hand Yellow Hand

Blue hand Yellow hand
Lie open on beach
Blue hand lifts tangle of kelp
Water drains away
Yellow hand caresses hip of bathing girl
Blue hand Yellow hand
Rest on offshore rocks
Water rises in a river to the sun

2 January 2015

The Moon, Swollen in Late Pregnancy

Moon swollen in late pregnancy,
Floats distractedly among cedars
Watched with curiosity by whispering stones
Who themselves drift on a current of broken light
As Old Woman
Who can explain it all
Sleeps dreamlessly in the darkness under the trees
The stones debate how matters have come to such a pass
While fragments of light sink through the viscera
Of the nearly forgotten towers that guard the forest
Their feet anchored securely in the memory of ancient wars
And the melodious mathematics of lost causes
Moon presses her hands to lift her heavy belly
And waits for Old Woman to awake
When she awakes Moon will inquire of her
How the light was shattered
What was at issue in the wars
That haunt the memories of the guardian towers
What will issue from her womb
What will become of the forest
After her blood and water irrigate its roots

September 2014

Passing through the Aspen Grove Beating Hand Drums

Passing through an aspen grove beating hand drums
The Singers wear shirts of white elk hide
The shirts are white as the aspen bark
The Singers descend in the night
Sent down by Moon
Moon Woman white as the aspen bark
Sends them down
The leaves are green
They will be yellow, they will be red
The Singers sing of the ancient wars
They sing of the blood that sank to the roots
The blood of the warriors
The blood of Moon Woman who gives birth
The leaves take the color of their blood
The leaves take the color of her blood
The leaves are green (now)

5 January 2015

A Nearly Full Moon Rising behind the Mountains

A nearly full moon rising behind the mountains
Casts doubt on all the philosophy that rises in mists from the lake
Where hover suspended in the deeper water discarded masks
And wasted opportunities .
Lying on one's back in the warm mud of the lake bottom
Looking upward through the dark water
Past the masks and the opportunities at the blurred image of the
  moon
One thinks of a red disk that lies on the bottom nearby
It vibrates with the passing of the breezes above
The letters inscribed on it are sometimes dark and sometimes bright
  and not always legible
It has been said that they mean this:

"The armies will march across the walls like pencil marks left by
  mice.
There is no reason why the sun cannot kneel and genuflect before
  the moon,
But she does not hold it against him that he does not.
Dragonflies nest in the hearts of dandelions,
Or dandelions in the hearts of dragonflies;
The experts disagree."

2 February 2015

Cut a Slit on the Surface of the Lake

Cut a slit on the surface of the lake
Pull back the sides like sheet rubber
Darkness bubbles up from the water
It stains the fingers
Ink to smear words on the walls of the cave
Where hide the daughters of the old woman who knows the stories
They huddle dispersed among the boxes
Baring glass teeth borrowed from glass foxes
That lurk in the brittle grass
That grows on the banks of the narrow river
It flows from the lake
It cuts deeper by the year through many-colored strata
Of petrified memory
Of musty garments discarded by the old woman's lovers
Of spiral stairwells with bannisters of foxes' vertebrae
That vanish at infinity
They have many landings along the way
On one sleeps the memory of a couple whose faces are unclear
Legs entangled in legs
A kiss on one breast
On the other an eye opening suddenly in surprise
It sees a vision of young deer
That frolic in a sunlit clearing unmindful of the scarlet battalions
That pass between them and around them like warm water through
     an enlacement of fingers
The young deer
They are those two children

Who disobediently stained their lips and tongues with the juice of
    a certain berry
And her lips became comely with rows of jewels
And he became the tower of David builded for an armoury
Meanwhile the scarlet battalions march down the narrow river
Through the many-colored strata and the heaps of discarded
    garments
Through the narrow canyon toward the cities of the plain

9 February 2015

On These Two Prongs of a Deer's Antler

On these two prongs of a deer's antler
Hang all the songs of the daughters
Who dwell in the labyrinths beneath the lake
They are legion
They hold between thumb and forefinger
Smooth clear stones
Each with a name written on it

WHITE MASK PEOPLE AND YELLOW MASK PEOPLE

White Mask People and Yellow Mask People
They appear in the aspen groves
Standing together in groups
Watching impassively from among the trees
The masks are oval-shaped and flat
With two slits for eyes and a slit for the mouth
The people are dressed in white tunics with long sleeves
They live in caverns deep in the earth
Where they sit on boxes
Never sleeping
Never needing sleep
They leave the caverns occasionally
To walk and stand among the aspen trees
And sometimes to drift between the moon and the sun
Remembering flights among the stars
One of them writes on the walls of a cavern
He writes by the light of shining stones
Embedded in the rock of the ceiling
He writes with a pen of raven quill
Dipped in the darkness that is stored in the boxes
The boxes are of cedar
It is very fragrant

A Woman Stands before an Open Window

A woman stands before an open window
A breeze agitates the folds of her gown
Her right arm hangs loose at her side holding a white mask
She watches the scarlet army marching through the valley below
I know that her breasts are free beneath the gown
I know the color of the aureoles
I am a music box on her dressing table
I am a seascape on her wall
I am a letter in the drawer of her escritoire
I am a spider hiding in a corner of the floor

2 February 2015

Beyond the Furthest Ridge

Beyond the farthest ridge
A door into summer
Mermaids pirouette on the linoleum in a patch of sunlight
Where an automobile mechanic lies sleeping curled like a crayfish
With my fingertips I feel the ridges and mountains on a map
Seeking a route for the rivers of desire that flow from beneath the
    temple
To give the mermaids a way to return to the sea

4 February 2015

A Giantess Peels Back the Skin of the Earth

A giantess peels back the skin of the earth with a fingernail
A clown's face grins through the opening
They are in collusion
To defraud of their virginity the girls who pass by fours through
    train stations
The girls' feet do not touch the floor
Though they are not as innocent as they seem
They have learned from old books the secrets the giantess will not
    share
They sometimes sit reading together in a garden in white wicker
    chairs
Enjoying the sunshine and comparing notes
The giantess enjoys immunity from prosecution for her frauds
That fact is noted in one of the books
In a caption to a line drawing
Illustrating the defeat of the legions of the last king
He is the clown who grins through the opening
Where the earth's skin is torn
The fingernail is long and is sometimes employed as a lingam
In an ancient worship of which the girls are secretly priestesses
How all this began is explained in the last chapter of a book of which
    they have heard
But in all their researches have not found

6 February 2015

At the End of the Evening

At the end of the evening the performers lay their folded costumes
    in the center ring
The ringmaster dallies with a sapphire that impersonates a hollow
    tree
The diagrams carved into its bark resemble sewing patterns
Printed on flimsy paper that aspires to a higher oblivion
The sapphire dissolves with a contented sigh
Its vapor clinging to the clothes of the ringmaster
All its tongues convulsing in unison to the whispers of the aban-
    doned costumes
The performers descend a jeweled stairway
That ends as a twist of yellow paper like a fly strip drawn out from
    its container
They will spend most of the night in wondering admiration of the
    diagrams

November 2014

THE UNDONE HAIR OF SATISFIED DESIRE

The undone hair of satisfied desire
Rises to the surface of the river
On a nearby hill workmen construct a watchtower
Of which each brick and board is a fragment of seer stone
Each stamped with a glyph translatable as I AM
It is to guard a sanctuary for penitent tax collectors of the late regime
A strand of hair is trapped in the mortar
But secretly plans to escape disguised as the neck ribbon of a visiting
    laundry girl
One of those who sleep in orderly formations beneath the bottom
    of the river
The weather is especially fine
Hammer blows resound in the summer air

October 2014

SEVEN TRAILS

On one trail from an opening in woods
A pool of clear water
In the depth a left arm clothed in the sleeve of a white gown
On the pointing finger a gold ring set with an emerald
Carved in the image of a moth

On the second a dying unicorn
Entrails spilled on the grass
And spangled with five-pointed stars red blue and silver

On the third a weathered shack with windows removed
Inside a bed with bare springs
A white porcelain pan upturned on the floor
A girl standing in the doorway
Hugging about her a blanket of moth wings

On the fourth a wrecked library
Books spilled in chaos on the floor
One open to a color plate of De Witte's "Morning Music"
A bouquet of daffodils in place of the pianist's head

On the fifth a steam locomotive abandoned on a stony beach

On the sixth a puppet stage
An enactment of the Book of Genesis in progress
To an audience of recently resurrected unicorns

On the seventh a door that opens to the touch
Releasing clouds of red blue and silver stars

October 2014

Quartet

The waters shall be healed
—Ezekiel 47:8

i

I stand in the hallway uncertain what to do. Today is the first day of classes—I am returning to university—and I know I have classes, but I have misplaced my schedule and do not know where to go. I see a door to what appears to be an office and go in to inquire. Several people are working in there, evidently mostly professors preparing to teach. There are many paper folders and ring binders with tabbed dividers. No one looks up at me. Then a woman approaches.

"Can I help you?" she says.

"Have you ever had that dream about knowing you have classes to attend, but you have lost your schedule and don't know where to go? I am having that experience now."

"Oh, dear. I will see what I can do."

She steps away, speaks to this person and that. Her dress is thin and clings to her hips and breasts. Meanwhile, I attempt to catch glimpses of the ring binders that lie open on the counters, hoping to see a clue to my own schedule. Finally I tire of waiting and return to the hallway. The hallway stretches before and behind me, with a fork going off to the right. They are more like underground tunnels. People walk purposefully in both directions, ignoring me. I feel tired and anxious. I know I have seen my schedule but cannot remember what is on it. A math class, I think, at ten o'clock, but where? I turn over the pages of the math text. It is new, printed on slick, expensive paper, but some pages are already stained. Someone has spilled cooking oil on one page, making a large, yellow stain that threatens to soak through to the next pages. Another page is puddled with pancake syrup; the pages might stick together, and I will be unable to learn what was on them.

I begin to think about finding a restroom. I look into one cubicle, but all the fixtures have been removed for remodeling. I look through another doorway, and at the end of a short entryway another door stands ajar revealing what looks like latrine holes in a crumbling stone bench, and shower heads. The latrine has been used and not cleaned. The floor feels spongy under my feet, and I am reluctant to walk on it. Everything looks old, worn, and of questionable cleanliness. I turn away. A few feet away a very tall, naked man stands, black hairs bristling over his whole body, but his facial features are indistinct. The man is holding a towel, evidently wanting to go in to take a shower. I carefully avoid making eye contact or looking at the man's privates and step past him back into the hallway

I think of the previous scenes and of my continuing need to find my class schedule as I drive an automobile on a narrowing road along a low ridge. The campus lies spread out below on my left. The road becomes muddy, then dead-ends at a patch of leafless brush. There is little room to turn around, but I back onto a crumbling shoulder, aware that it might give way at any moment; and it does, causing the automobile to slip backward and downward, stopped by heavy brush. I need to get back to campus to look for my classes. I am aware that the woman in the office is skeptical of my performance so far.

The summer I was twelve years old my parents rented a cabin in pine woods for a week. The air was hot and the smell of the pines was strong. There was a small lake with lily pads and fish. One day I went exploring about the edge of the lake, which was surrounded by pine trees. At the far side of the lake I stepped out of the tree line onto the edge of a field of dried stubble. At the center of the field, about a football field's length away, was a small house. I walked to it, seeing as I neared it that it was old, built of gray, weathered, unpainted wood. There was no glass in the windows, and the door hung on one hinge. I smelled the sun-heated wood. I looked in through a window at what plainly had been the kitchen. The sink and stove had been removed, but there was an old table, and a white granite pan overturned on the floor, and scraps of newspaper. I could see through another door into a room where a metal bed frame sat against the far wall. A piece of red and white checkered oil cloth covered something on the window ledge. I moved the oil cloth aside and saw what I thought was the top of the head of a little goat with nubbins of horns, mounted on a wooden plaque like a trophy. I rubbed the little horns and felt the rough white hair. I pulled the cover back over the little trophy and thought of going inside the house, but I thought it better not to. Years later, as I remember this incident, I think on how unlikely is the part about the goat's head, but I am certain it happened.

That memory returns to me vividly as I climb out of the automobile onto the muddy embankment to consider how to get the automobile back onto the road. The woman from the office stands motionless and silent a few yards from the house, to my left. Her dress clings to the front of her body.

ii

Looking down from balcony on second level of shopping mall
Well lighted
Benches
Flashes of gold and green
People moving through
Fluorescent orange underclothing behind plate glass
Dark up here, lights out

Someone behind
Two or three
One dark form in peripheral vision
Rumor in the air:
A shooter in the mall
Moving closer
People continue moving through unconcerned
Should find cover
Try door handle
Unlocked
Dark empty shoe store
Pass between display racks
Door open into lighted room at back
Woman sitting naked on edge of narrow bed with back to door
Turns head slightly to right
"Come in," she says
A drawer slides open at the small of her back
So long since seeing her
A pang of hope
Ask her, "Have you returned to stay?"
"Touch me not," she says
Look into drawer
A revolver
Walking with her on balcony
Hand in hand
Revolver in other hand
"I'm not dressed," she says
"Someone might see me"
She covers her sex with the empty drawer
Why did she say "touch me not"?
Walking together on balcony
Her face is carved wood

Motion to right
Turn quickly pointing revolver
In woods on river bank
She has ascended

Revolver in hand
Motion to right
Cartridges are pencils and sticks

iii

The soft flesh of the moon has little in common with the slack-faced
    caricatures
Of minor dictators that appear so often painted on department store
    display windows
The next election might reverse this condition
But for the time being it must be endured
Along with the chains of paper dolls dressed in police uniforms
That festoon all the bridges on the way to City Hall
I, a painter of those caricatures, contemplate that prospect
As I sit with legs dangling over the edge of a bridge
With an arm hooked firmly around a steel girder
But my mind wanders
I would prefer to be painting pictures of a woman I saw as I
    approached the bridge
I saw her only from behind
Dressed in a black sheath with a long zipper down the back
She walked on to the other side of the river
High heels clicking
Hips moving pleasingly beneath the fabric of the dress
Nylon stockings scattering glints of morning sun
Leaving behind her a profusion of musical notation like a cloud of
    mosquitos

And a faint sweet odor of freshly dry-cleaned police uniforms
I suspect that her unseen face is a tear-gas canister set in a cluster
    of daffodils
I find this thought arousing
In a few minutes my daily regimen will require me to return to my
    studio
Necessitating a walk down that long boulevard bordered on both
    sides by vendors of broken wagon wheels
Fast-food restaurants
Empty lots overgrown with milkweed and marsh grass
(I confess to enjoying the pungent odor of the milkweed
Which reminds me of the wife of my youth)
Conjurers' supply shops
Opera houses
Museums of erotic toys
A library specializing in works on eighteenth-century Rumanian
    alchemy
A museum housing a simulation of the surface of the moon
Where children can experience walking on the peculiar sponginess
    of its flesh
A munitions factory where all the workers are young females cross-
    trained in the art of Egyptian rug weaving
(Their teeth are recycled piano keys)
A retirement home for disabled poachers
Great heaps of shed puff-adder skins often utilized as wall paper for
    the poor
Or the fabric of costumes for performers in the opera houses
Vendors of antique election campaign buttons
The variety is endless and constantly changing
I find it all tedious
The walk might be somewhat less tedious
If I could anticipate an assignation at the studio with the woman
    in the black dress

But I know in my heart that if I embrace her
Her torso will collapse into an armful of splintered violins
When I arrive at the studio later that morning however
I am consoled by finding a tear gas canister on my doorstep
And a bouquet of daffodils in the pot that holds my paint brushes

October 2014

iv

When I see her next she is standing in the little house
In the field of dried stubble
Her back still turned toward me
Her black sheath dress unzipped
And slipped down off her left shoulder
Exposing the skin of her torso
The drawer has moved up from the small of her back
And is drawn open from her left rib cage
I step through the doorway and approach cautiously
She does not speak or move
In the drawer I see a key
Which I carefully withdraw
Then stand wondering what it will open
And though I do not see her face
I know it is hidden by a white mask
With slits for the eyes and mouth
Through the window beyond her
A procession of children appears from the edge of the woods
And begins to approach slowly
Very slowly, weeks will pass between steps
Hearing the sound of water
I turn to look out the door, holding the key
And see that a spring has begun to flow from beneath the floor

It becomes a stream that carves a channel into the soft earth of the
    field
It soon deepens and I see the many strata of rock beneath
Orange and cream and black and red
The smell of hot stone under the noon sun permeates the air
As the river rushes downward through the canyon
Toward the warm salt sea that lies with its knees raised in the abyss
    below
Waiting to be healed
And I reach up and insert the key into the sun

December 2014

WALL ATTEMPTS TO COVER ITS BREASTS

Wall attempts to cover its breasts with songs of breaking glass
Man in Stetson puts head through noose and grins
Tiny fragments of glass shower him with praise
"Let some words be yours alone," he says
Wall folds, hides in corner with unendurable shame
Head falls off man in Stetson
Stetson's crown is breast of wall
"Hoard them, treasure them"

September 2014

A Boy Sits at a Table

A boy sits at a table in an immense library filled with shelves of large and heavy books. In these books are all the secrets that forever draw us on and forever elude us. Before him on a table a book lies open and inviting him to read, and he reads, but afterward he remembers only fragments of sentences, even of words: "the key that unlocks the door of," "ington has painted," "ewise," "a girl's shoe lying in the hallway."

AUTHOR'S NOTE

Most of my likely readers will find the poems in the first part of this collection, approximately through "Outside the Longhouse," to be readily accessible, but those in the latter part of the book may seem puzzling and strange—"surrealistic," though I am not a Surrealist (Neo-Romanticist influenced by Surrealism is closer to the mark). If the reader finds a beauty in those poems, despite their seeming irrationality, and though it be a mysterious beauty, then I call them successful. My method for composing them has been an exercise of something like what Keats called "negative capability," which I understand as a stepping back of the conscious, controlling mind with its categories and preconceptions to allow the poem to emerge from "somewhere else." It is similar to Mallarmé's method, and also the Surrealists', as described by Wallace Fowlie: "To give over all initiative to the words themselves" *(Mallarmé,* Phoenix Books, 1962). I suggest that they be approached as dreams. Every reader will have had the experience of waking with a dream that seems important and meaningful, though the full meaning might remain elusive. Some of the imagery in these poems, in fact, came from sleeping dreams. Most of them, however, are more like waking dreams. I view dreams as messages from a deeper part of our being, the "unconscious," if you will, supplying insights to assist us in the conscious conduct of life. I entertain the possibility that such messages are revelatory in a certain sense, for they come from a place within us that, by God's grace, is uncorrupted by the Fall. The unconscious always speaks the truth of its insights and evaluations about matters on which at the conscious level "the natural man," as it is called in the Book of Mormon (Mosiah 3:19), is too willing to equivocate, rationalize, and deny. The "I" in the mortal conscious mind wants to cheat, but the unconscious is unfailingly honest. Whether messages from my unconscious are of value to anyone but me, the reader will decide, but my sense is that my life's tasks are not wholly unlike those of others, and I become more persuaded to the Jungian view that a common set of archetypal figures from a collective unconscious speaks in dreams to us all, and, because we share the "human condition," what is spoken to one might be of value to another. As Joseph Campbell has put it, "Myths are public dreams; dreams are private myths." I would add that the public myth must begin in someone's private myth.

More can be said about the nature of these oneiric poems (which is what I prefer they be called), but to say it with anything approaching completeness requires far more philosophical and theological verbiage than space available here permits, and to condense it renders it even more incoherent than it is in fuller discourse. Nevertheless, I think I must say something, and it is the following: to my mind, poems of this kind can be merest glimpses through a window on the infinite and eternal and marvelous and rationally, literally unspeakable mystery of being, of "that which is Spirit, even the Spirit of truth," in the words of Joseph Smith (Doctrine and Covenants 93:23); of the utter freedom—agency—of Being; of the erotic and convulsively beautiful ecstasy of Eternal Life and Creation.

Biographical Note

Colin Blaine Douglas was born in 1944 and brought up in Western
Washington; is an enrolled member of the Samish Indian Nation; be-
came a Latter-day Saint at the age of sixteen; served in the Brazilian
Mission in 1964–1966; served in Military Intelligence in the Regu-
lar Army and the Utah National Guard, retiring as a sergeant first
class; attended the University of Washington as a journalism major
and received a bachelor's degree in psychology and a master's degree
in American literature at Brigham Young University; was employed
for twenty years as an editor in the Curriculum Department of The
Church of Jesus Christ of Latter-day Saints; edited and reported for
the *Magna* (Utah) *Times* newspaper for two years; with the former
Linda Jean Wells, to whom he was married in 1969, is the father
of seven; has resided in Utah since 1971; as literary favorites names
Latter-day Saint scripture (including the Bible), Arthur Rimbaud,
André Breton, Ezra Pound, T. S. Eliot, Kenneth Rexroth, Gary Sny-
der, and Philip Lamantia.

Acknowledgments

"I sought you, Adonai," *Ensign*, Oct. 1979

"Let the stone whisper to the flower," *Dialogue* 13.4 (1980)

"Like a deer he comes to me," *Dialogue* 13.4 (1980); *Harvest: Contemporary Mormon Poems*, ed. Eugene England and Dennis Clark (Salt Lake City: Signature Books, 1989)

"My beloved shall be mine beyond death," *Ensign*, Feb. 1981

"A daughter of Sarah is my beloved," *Sunstone* 8.6 (1983)

"Adonai: cover me with your robe," *Sunstone* 10.10 (1986); *Harvest* (1989)

"Wedding songs," *Sunstone* 10.10 (1986); *Harvest* (1989)

"Let the grasses sing," *Sunstone* 10.10 (1986)

"Adonai: I have sinned" and "Adonai: forsake me not," *Sunstone* 12.1 (1988)

"Prayer," *Irreantum*, 2006